Dada Duh!

A Simple Method for Enjoying an Art Show

**Written and Illustrated
by
Grace Lehto**

Written and Illustrated
by
Grace Lehto

ISBN-13: 978-0-9858520-0-9

Sincere appreciation and many thanks to Michael Havelin,
mystery author and friend, who patiently and wisely
helped me prepare this book for publication.
I could not have done it without him.

Published by   **Grace Kellie Publishing**
PO Box 16675
Asheville, NC 28870

Table of Contents

Introduction

About the title: Dada was an art movement that began around 1916 at the end of World War I. It was meant as a protest against inhumanity and the lack of order in post-war Germany and was often disorganized in a purposeful way. Hans Arp, for instance, made a series of collages by dropping pieces of paper on a larger piece of paper and then glued them down wherever they happened to land.

Dada poets would cut words from newspapers and magazines and put them in a bag, shake them up and pull them out one by one and then publish the result as poetry.

When I first began to realize that I am an artist, I thought about all the different "isms" that separate "art" into movements. I like the sound of "Dada." Sometimes it seems to me that it expresses much of what I see in museums and art shows. Like why did they even bother to frame that thing?

I wanted to present a book that would help people look at art without having to know all this stuff about "isms" and make an art show fun for nearly anyone. Thus the title, "Dada, Duh!"

So yes, this is a book about art.

It is not about how to make art, but rather how to look at art. It is not meant for artists, critics and sophisticated aficionados who already know a lot about art and can probably rattle off twenty names of artistic movements without blinking an eye.

This is a book for ordinary people such as yourself (and me, too) who occasionally drop into an art museum. Perhaps to meet someone. On the other hand, because there's a special exhibit, or maybe even to get out of the rain.

If you are like me, you may have complained about the things you have seen hanging on the walls in galleries and museum exhibits. You are confused. Moreover, when you try to express this confusion, you've been confronted with subtle and sometimes not-so-subtle put-downs. You may have been called provincial, unsophisticated or culturally deprived.

This book will not explain the Art that you've found so confusing. Come on, red paint dripped on a bread wrapper and glued to a rusty fender? Let's get real here. This is a game of the Emperor's New Clothes methinks. I have no explanation for some of the things they actually enshrine in the museums.

Now, there are all kinds of names for different schools of art. There's Baroque, Classicism, Neo-Classicism, Realism, Impressionism, Expressionism, Fauvism, Cubism, Futurism, Surrealism, Abstractionism, Abstract Surrealism, Surrealistic Abstractionism, Dadaism, Neo-Dadaism, Pop Art and Minimalism, not to mention Conceptual Art. And that's not all. Confusing, right? How do you keep them all straight?

Not to worry. I've got good news for you! There are really only four categories of visual art. Just four. Nice and easy. Check them out listed below

- Category 1: Controlled somethingness

- Category 2: Uncontrolled somethingness

- Category 3: Controlled nothingness

- Category 4: Uncontrolled nothingness

Remember these four groups. (There will be a quiz later.) I will also explain how some of the schools of art fit into these categories.

This basic four-part framework can make a trip to an art show fun. Four basic categories of art. At last, a way to look at that stuff and say something besides, "it doesn't compute."

Additionally in one easy lesson you will learn how to speak the language of the art critic and graduate from provincial to culturally aware. My sure fire system will have you talking like you know all about art in just a few days. There are quizzes at the end of each section to help you learn the lingo.

An added feature is a section to give you guidance should you decide to purchase a piece of original art for any reason whatsoever whether you have a hole in the wall you want to cover, or have a starving artist friend, or wish to impress a date.

Chapter One

The Basic Four

Category 1 – Controlled Somethingness

Sometimes when I walk into an exhibit, it's visual cacophony. So much to look at, so much to see. But it IS manageable if you concentrate on one work at a time.

The first thing you have to ask yourself is "What is this?" Is it a picture of a person, place or thing that exists in reality? If your answer is yes, then you are already halfway to the correct category. It is somethingness. Now for the second half. Is the piece you are contemplating an attempt to create three dimensional reality on a two dimensional surface or is it blurry and lopsided where you can still recognize it as "something"?

If it seems that the effort of the artist was focused on execution and an accurate portrayal of actuality, it can be called "Controlled Somethingness" or Category One.

Think of Norman Rockwell or Andrew Wyeth. Michelangelo or Rubens. These are artists whose works are sometimes classified as Realists, Neo-realists, Paintings of flowers, a still life with fruit, an ocean view are also Category One.

Surrealists such as Max Ernst and Salvador Dali are also Controlled Somethingness. While the works they produced are not reality, they present a unified image that draws on

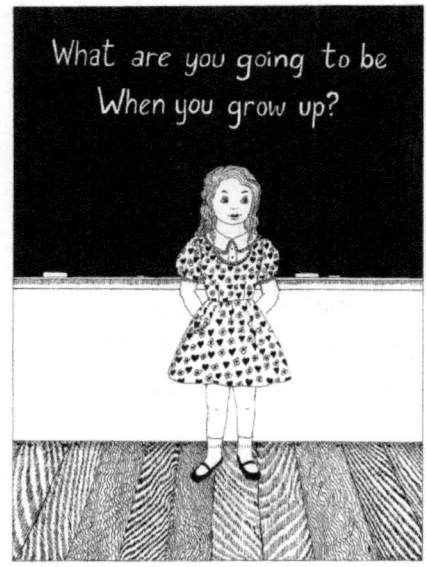

reality and is a juxtaposition of elements that are recognizable.

This is Controlled Somethingness. You can recognize it as something from reality. It is an illustration in pen and ink for a book entitled "What I'm Gonna Do When I'm Queen." Notice the wood grain on the floor and the pattern on the girl's dress. There is a lot of detail here.

Please note that all the illustrations for this book are done by the author to save money and paperwork in an attempt to garner the proper permissions required to avoid prosecution for copyright infringement.

Category 2 – Uncontrolled Somethingness

Category 2 includes Expressionism, neo-expressionism, Impressionism and is again from reality. However, the finished work does not emphasize visual reality but the artist's interpretation of reality. Think of Van Gogh's "Starry Night" or "Guernica" by Picasso. Degas and Monet also come to mind. The images are recognizable but the focus is on the message or observation of the artist about the reality he or she sees. "The Scream" by Edvard Munch would be a prime example of Uncontrolled Somethingness.

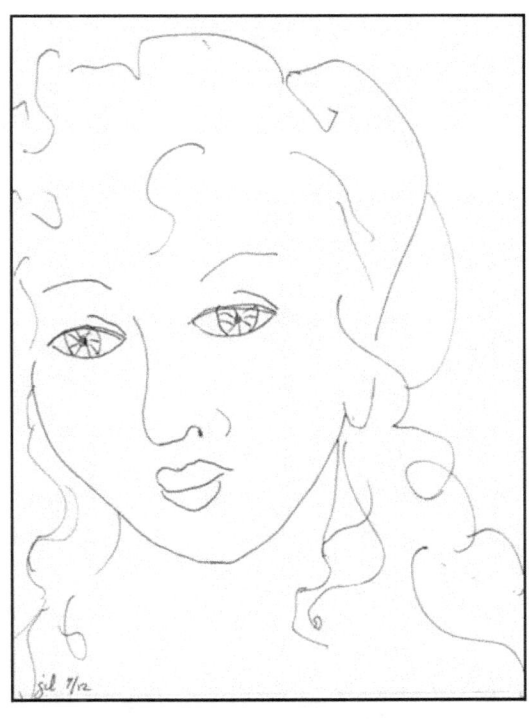

This category also includes the rough sketches made by artists as they plan a more elaborate work or jot down an idea for a later work. Cartoons and caricatures would be included in this group as well.

Here, you can recognize that this is the face of a woman. Very few lines, but you can see what it is. It certainly does not seem to have much "control." In fact, it has a "loose" feel to it. It is a sketch for another, more detailed, more controlled painting.

Category 3 – Controlled Nothingness

When you see one of these pieces, you may wonder what it is at the same time you can appreciate the amount of effort that has obviously been expended to create whatever it is.

This category, often skillfully executed, represents nothing that exists. Geometric forms, tangles of lines, dots in a pattern. The work may be visually interesting and even remind you of something but it does not seem to stem from objective reality. Mondrian made square blocks of color. Sometimes it's circles within circles or the interplay of triangles. It can be almost anything as long as it's nothing recognizable from everyday life. Intricate curving lines, or stair steps that lead to nothing as in the work of MC Escher. Aubrey Beardsley's intricate black and white designs also fall into Category 3.

If art is a means of communication, it is sometimes difficult to understand the message of the artist. I remember once seeing a giant canvas that was four feet tall, eight feet wide and painted entirely green. "What," I thought, "is that?" I peeked at the placard next to the painting. It was entitled "Lawn" and that helped me to understand, or at least consider the message of the artist. Perhaps it was someone who loved spring and green lawns so much they could only express their enthusiasm for it by making it BIG. Or it was an artist who was sick and tired of mowing the dang lawn because it seemed like a gargantuan task. Possibly, it was an artist frustrated with his or her inability to grow a perfect lawn of consistent color and devoid of weeds and this painting was the ideal to which their lawn was held. Still, the placard gave me a clue, a framework for consideration of the piece.

Category 3 pieces can often be evocative of emotions or revelatory of the nature of shape and shadow. Optical illusions are often included in this group of work as well.

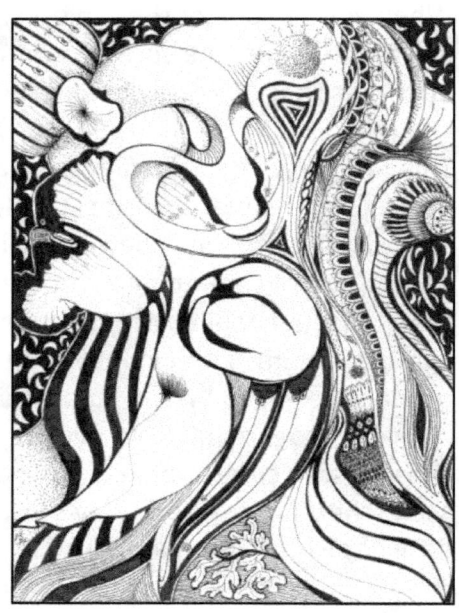

This is Controlled Somethingness; Category 3. Look at the amount of detail. Certainly controlled but representative of nothing in reality.

Category 4 – Uncontrolled Nothingness

This category is easy to spot. It is not a depiction of anything you see in reality. In addition, it seems casual, knocked off, done in a trice. Think of Jackson Pollack's splatter paintings. Or the works of parrots, chimpanzees and three year olds. I remember watching a documentary of Jackson Pollack's work one time. On the floor, a canvass was rolled out for nearly fifty feet. The artist had a ladder and worked his way across the long span dropping paint from above onto the canvass in a random manner. When the surface was covered with paint and eventually dry, Mr. Pollack cut out sections he liked for framing.

Some of the works in this category display interesting movements of the brush or exciting color combinations. The pieces often used in interior decoration as a splash of color or an accent against a contrasting wall.

I usually produce work in this category when I have a new medium to work with. Will it blend? Can I erase it? Are the colors strong or pale? What happens if I mix it with soap? Is it opaque or transparent? How long does it take to dry? Does it smudge? A new medium is exciting to me and I like to know what it will do. The result of such messing around is definitely Category 4, Uncontrolled Nothingness.

All of the work I present here is pen and ink. This is from cleaning my pen one day. It represents nothing and is Uncontrolled Nothingness. But I did get my pen clean.

Chapter 1 - Quiz – Categories of Art

Instructions:

Do not worry. This will be an open book test. (Really, how could it be anything else? You've gotta have the book open to read the questions). Should a breeze blows across the pages and happens to open to the page that answers the question, well I guess that's just good luck.

Please circle the answer you believe to be correct. If you wish to pass this book along, you might like to do it in pencil or to write your answers on a separate sheet of paper numbered 1 thru 10. A separate piece of paper will also make it easier to check your answers found in the back of the book.

Let the testing begin:

1. Category 1 (Controlled Somethingness) might also be called...

   a. Realistic portrayal of an actual scene, object or person.

   b. A picture of something

   c. Identifiable

   d. All of the above

   e. A and C only.

2. Category 3 (Controlled Nothingness) is
   a. Usually a landscape painting
   b. Always realistic
   c. Not recognizable as anything that exists
   d. A and B
   e. C and B
   f. All of the above

3. Category 4 (Uncontrolled Nothingness) is
   a. Nearly the same as Category 1
   b. Nearly the opposite of Category 1
   c. The favorite technique of Norman Rockwell
   d. None of the above
   e. All of the above

4. Category 2 (Uncontrolled Somethingness)
   a. It is a picture of something.
   b. It is closely related to Category 1
   c. Can be an artist's impression of reality
   d. All of the above.
   e. A and C only.

5. The following illustration is

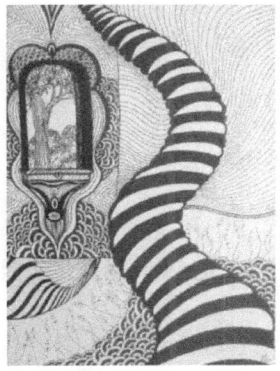

    a. Category 1

    b. Category 2

    c. Category 3

    d. Category 4

6. Below is a drawing from which category?

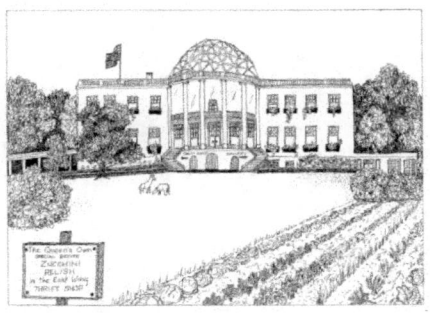

    a. Controlled Somethingness

    b. Uncontrolled Somethingness

    c. Uncontrolled Nothingness

    d. Controlled Nothingness

7. Which Category is also called "Controlled Nothingness"

    a. Category 1

    b. Category 2

    c. Category 3

    d. Category 4

8. Uncontrolled Somethingness is also known as

    a. Category 1

    b. Category 2

    c. Both a. and b.

    d. Neither a. nor b.

9. Select the illustration that falls into

Category 4

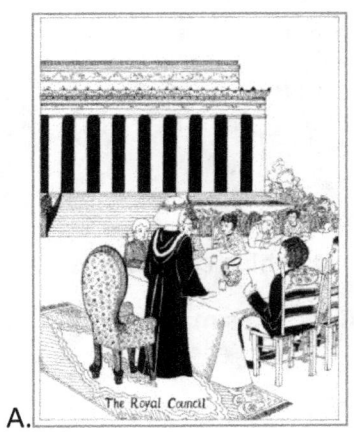

A.

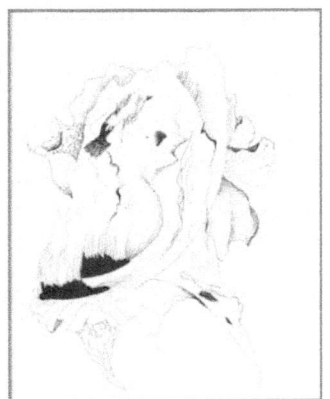

B.

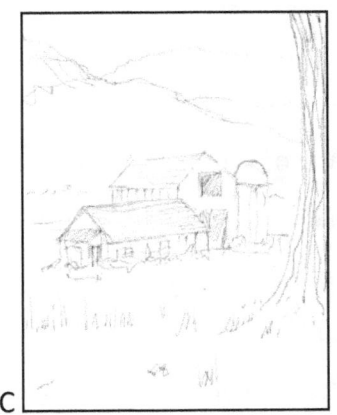

C

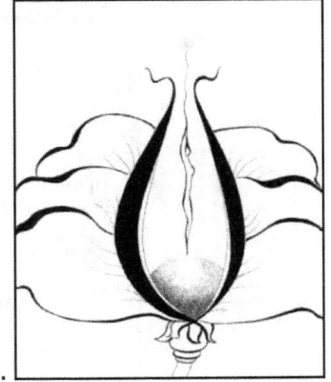

D.

10. In which category or categories can you find an image that exists in reality?

    a. Category B and D

    b. Category A and B

    c. Category C only.

    d. Category C and D

11. For your bonus point, which category do you like the best? Choose as many as you like.

    a. Category A

    b. Category B

    c. Category C

    d. Category D

    e. I don't like any of them.

    f. I like them all.

    g. Category A and B

    h. Category C and D

    i. I'd like it better in color.

    j. Art is a means of communication.

    k. I don't get it.

    l. Art is good for the soul.

    m. I wish I could draw.

Chapter 2

Talking Art

I am sure you've heard politicians ramble on with patriotic phrases that don't really mean much. Well, I think they're all using Buzz Phrase Generators. They've got these lists of words that they put together and toss out a few of them strung together to make some patriotic sounds while they actually are not saying much at all.

To my knowledge, no one has ever done one for the art world, so here goes.

There will be three lists of words of ten words each in this Art Speak Buzz Phrase Generator numbered 0 thru 9 .with a phonetic guide for each word. No definitions will be included because it is not important to know what you are saying, only that it sounds important and is pronounced correctly.

Adverbs

0. Quintessentially – **(**kwint-e-**sen**-sha-lee)
1. Distinctively – (dis-**tink**-tiv-lee)
2. Dynamically – (die-**nam**-ik-lee)
3. Essentially – (es-**sen**-sha-lee)
4. Aesthetically – (as-**thet**-ik-lee)
5. Excitingly – (x-**site**-ing-lee)
6. Artistically – (r-**tist**-ik-lee)
7. Principally – (**prin**-sip-lee)
8. Manneristically – (man-ur-**is**-tik-lee)
9. Eloquently – (**el**-oh-kwent-lee)

Please note that I made up this pronunciation guide using my own notations. Many dictionary publishers copyright their methodology and in order to avoid getting myself in trouble, I invented the system I am using.

Please feel free to substitute other words in the future. Just make sure that they have as many syllables as possible in order to impress your listeners and let them know for sure that you are highly informed. You may even decide to make up your own Buzz Phrase Generator for another topic.

I realize that those who write about art can sometimes be hard pressed to express their reactions to the works they write about and I am not accusing them of ever, ever using a device such as I am revealing to you now. Actually, I don't pay much attention to critics and what they have to say. I have my own sense of what appeals to me and I insist on following my own preferences.

Adjectives

0. Translucent – (tranz-**loo**-sent)
1. Eclectic – (ek-**lek**-tik)
2. Esoteric – (es-o-**ter**-ik)
3. Egalitarian – (e-gal-a-**tare**-e-an)
4. Quixotic – (kwix-**ot**-ik)
5. Qualitative – (kwal-e-**tay**-tiv)
6. Didactic – (di-**dak**-tik)
7. Ethereal – (eth-**er**-E-el)
8. Innovative – (in-no-**vay**-tiv)
9. Explorative – (x-**plor**-a-tiv)

If you take the trouble to learn and use some of these words, you will be able to confuse the most erudite art expert in the world. If, for instance someone says to you, "What do you mean?" Simply reply, "Well, if you'd like me to break it down for you…" This will usually stop them in their tracks.

If, however, they decide to press you further with another question, you might want to respond with some statement like "in one syllable words, I do (or do not) really find this piece appealing."

This Buzz Phrase Generator will allow you to attend any show, gallery opening or museum with the confidence that no one can question your impeccable taste.

Nouns

0. Composition – (kom-poe-**zish**-un)
1. Manifestation – (man-i-fes-**tay**-shun)
2. Perspective – (per-**spek**-tiv)
3. Assemblage – (as-**sem**-blige)
4. Dimensionality – (duh-men-shun-**al**-eh-tee)
5. Work – (work)
6. Presentation – (pree-zen-**tay**-shun)
7. Preparation – (prep-er-**ay**-shun)
8. Construction – (kon-**struk**-shun)
9. Exhibition – (x-eh-**bish**-un)

Another ten words presented here for your edification. With the exception of but one word, they are all at least three syllables in length. That word (Number 5) is "work" which is, as you know, a four-letter word. Tsk, tsk.
Below is a table to make it easier for you to put phrases together and start impressing your friends and acquaintances.

	Adverbs	Adjectives	Nouns
0	Quintessentially	Translucent	Composition
1	Distinctively	Eclectic	Manifestation
2	Dynamically	Esoteric	Perspective
3	Essentially	Egalitarian	Assemblage
4	Aesthetically	Quixotic	Dimensionality
5	Excitingly	Qualitative	Work
6	Artistically	Didactic	Presentation
7	Principally	Ethereal	Preparation
8	Manneristically	Innovative	Construction
9	Eloquently	Explorative	Exhibition

And here is how to use this thing: Say you're standing in front of a piece in an art show and someone asks you what you think. You say "It's definitely a distinctively quixotic assemblage." That phrase is number 1-4-3.

Try it yourself. Phrase number 6-0-7 is an artistically translucent preparation. Got it? I hope so, because the quiz comes next. And this time, the quiz is not so much about what you've learned, but a way to practice and become familiar with the words you can use to express your knowledge and expertise of the field of art.

And yes, it is still an open book test and the answers are in the back of the book. If you still have that piece of paper you used for the first quiz, here's your opportunity to add to it. I hope you started out with a fairly sizeable sheet because there are more quizzes to come. And a final test at the end.

Chapter 2 Quiz - Talking About Art

1. What number is the phrase "Manneristically ethereal exhibition?
   a. 2-1-3
   b. 8-8-9
   c. 8-7-9
   d. 4-5-6

2. How many phrases can be made with a Buzz Phrase Generator?
   a. 173
   b. 1000
   c. 100
   d. 10

3. The phrase 2-3-9 is
   a. Distinctively qualitative dimensionality
   b. Dynamically egalitarian composition
   c. Dynamically egalitarian exhibition
   d. Excitingly didactic perspective

4. What phrase number is principally esoteric work?
   a. 9-7-3
   b. 3-3-9
   c. 2-2-5
   d. 7-2-5

5. What phrase number is quintessentially explorative manifestation?
   a. 0-8-3
   b. 0-2-1
   c. 0-9-1
   d. 0-9-3

6. Complete the following sentence with two phrases from your generator. (I suggest you actually write out the words instead of the numbers so that you may familiarize yourself with the vocabulary.)

I find that the _____ _____

_____ is indicative of a _____

_____ _____.

7. Another bonus question. Please select all that apply.
    a. I feel confident that I can use these words.
    b. I am still confused.
    c. Why would I do this?
    d. This can be fun.
    e. I look forward to the next art show.
    f. I found a mistake.
    g. I'm putting this book in the next garage sale.
    h. I like the quizzes.
    i. None of the above
    j. All of the above.
    k. B and D only.

Chapter 3

Buying Art

There are lots of reasons you might want to get some art to hang on your walls.

- Perhaps you have a hole in the wall you want to cover or an ugly stain from the time you threw a glass of red wine at your cheating partner.

- You have a friend who is an artist. You want to support his/her efforts.

- You want to impress people. Let them know you have some real culture.

- You need something to complete your décor. Your walls look bare.

- You want to make an investment and want to make a good return on your money.

- You see a painting that you keep going back to look at. You really like it and cannot seem to get it out of your head.

The Hole in the Wall Problem

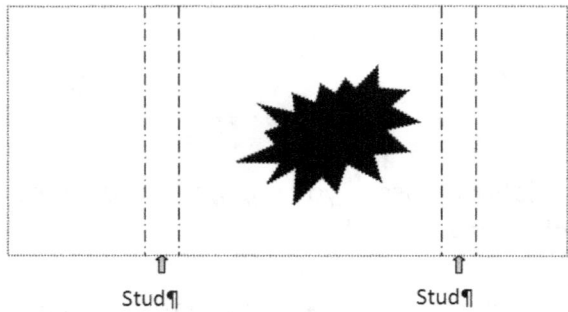

Stud¶   Stud¶

OK. You were moving the furniture and the lamp got pushed through the wall. Or you were having a party and it got a little rowdy. Whatever. But there you are with a hole. And you need to cover it before your parents or your boss come to dinner.

First, measure the hole. The artwork you hang should exceed the size of the hole by at least two inches in all directions.

Secondly, locate the studs. These are the pieces of wood to which your drywall or paneling are nailed. They are usually 16 inches apart and if you have trouble locating them then you can purchase a stud finder (and I'm not talking about a sexy dress). Ask the guy (or gal) at your local hardware store and he'll show you what you need. You have several options to consider in selection of your camouflage artwork.

You will need to decide which stud you will use to hang your painting. The stud will be at the center of your painting and must be wide enough to cover the hole.

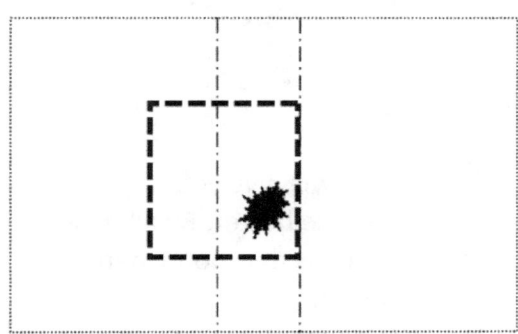

How far from the stud is the opposite side of the hole? Let say it's 8 inches from the center of the hole to the furthest edge of the hole. That means you're your painting will need to extend about two inches beyond the furthest edge of the hole or about ten inches from the center of the stud. (2 + 8 = 10). So your painting should be about twenty inches wide. The height of the painting will need to be a total of four inches taller than the hole. I've drawn some options here so you can get an idea of the possibilities.

Here's a larger painting that certainly covers the hole and dominates the wall. You might was to consider something like this if you have a lot of space and not much furniture. Maybe it got busted up at that rowdy party.

How about a gigantic oval? This may be just the thing if you're into a romantic Victorian feel in your décor.

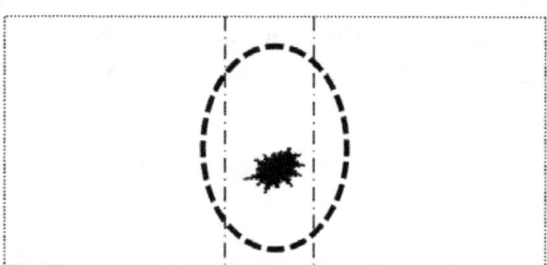

Don't forget the other stud. This will give you a different placement and may suit your space better. By all means take the color and lighting into consideration when selecting your fine art camouflage.

Use both studs to hang your purchase. If you go for this

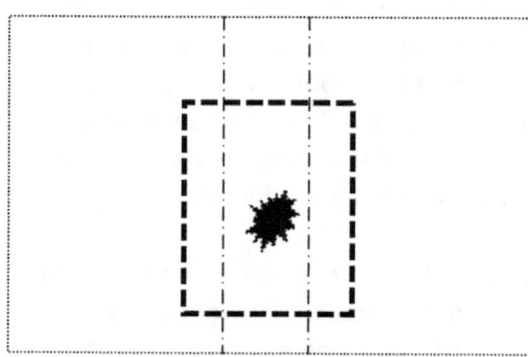

option, the painting you hang will need to be at least 20 inches wide. Make sure that the nails on each stud are the same height.

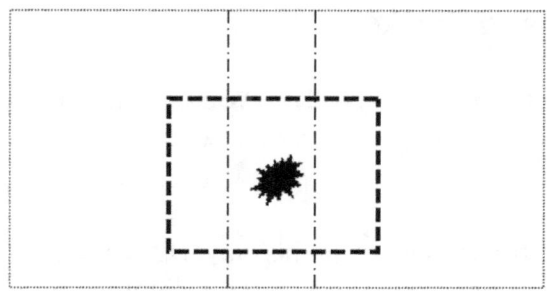

If you don't like art and don't want to hang a painting, I question your sanity. Why are you reading this book? Nonetheless you still do have other options. You can patch the wall, move the furniture to cover the hole, or leave town the day before your parents and/or boss are due to arrive.

So, your relatives or the boss or some other person who is not high on your list of likeableness showed up and instead of a hole in the wall, you have a blood stain from finally putting them out of their misery. My first suggestion is that you just replace the wall. What with the forensic possibilities these days, you'll never be able to escape

detection. (If you've seen the same TV shows that I have, the teensiest little speck can do you in.) If the blood has pooled on the floor, you will need a large, very heavy 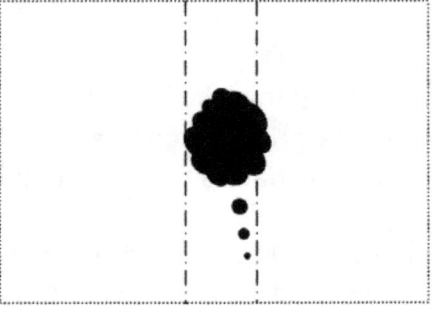 sculpture to cover it up. Whatever you do, do not try to stuff the body in the wall. For efficient body disposal, you will have to consult with someone else. I've never had the problem.

Your Friend the Artist

Sam's a helluva guy, he really is. You have been friends for years and for as long as you've known him he's been an artist.

Now, hard times have come his way. His work isn't selling and galleries typically take a 35 -50% commission if they take his work at all. His rent is due and he's been eating ramen noodles for the past two weeks.

Course, he won't be getting royalties. Unlike a musician, an actor or a writer, once his work is sold, it's gone. If someone buys a painting from him for say $1000 and then later sells it for $20,000, he will never see a penny of the profit. There are states where artists are awarded 5% of the price increase whenever a work is resold. However, it's nothing Sam can count on.

Before you buy something from Sam, ask yourself these questions?

- Do you like his work?
- Do you think he has talent?
- Is the price reasonable?
- Do you have a place to put it?

If you sincerely like his work, if it really appeals to you, then you should do your best to support his efforts. If you don't like his work, have you ever told him so? Sure, Sam is your friend but is he enough of a friend that you can tell him the truth? If you don't like his work and you've never told him that in all the years you've known him, you're being dishonest.

There are plenty of ways to tell him without being cruel. You could say, "Your work just doesn't appeal to me." That's better than saying, "I think it's fucking ugly crap." (If that's how you really feel, you've been totally dishonest and a cad to boot.) If you really don't think he has talent, send him brochures for trade schools and leave the want ads on his kitchen table. Just be nice about it.

It is possible to think he has talent and not like his work. Me, I'm a Pollyanna and like to look at the bright side. Negative stuff does not appeal to me. Paintings of murder and death may be well done, innovative, and well executed, but I don't want them in my home. Personal preference. So if you think he has talent and don't like his work, pass on buying a painting and think of other ways to help him out. Talk to people who might be able to host a show. Introduce Sam to others who might like his work. And by all means put together box of canned food and drop it off when you go to take him out to dinner.

Sam may have an over-inflated idea of the price he can charge. He wants $20,000 for a pencil sketch of a stick figure. If you like it, negotiate. If not, then don't buy it. As a friend, you should try to talk to him a bit about the reality of his pricing structure. If you believe that he may eventually be able to pay you back, you could offer him a loan. Just don't loan him anything you can't afford to lose. And if you can afford $20,000 for a pencil sketch of a stick figure, please give me a call. Have I got some deals for you!

Finally, like I said, you've known Sam for years. You may already have enough of his work to cover every square inch of wall space. Bear in mind that when Sam comes over for a visit, he's going to expect to see his work hanging in a place of prominence. Do you have a place to put it? If not, what will you do with it if you buy it? If you truly don't have space for it, it's time to tell Sam that you cannot possibly buy his work until you move.

It's wonderful if you can help a friend in whom you believe. It is foolish to be his sole source of support. Your first priority should be to take care of yourself. After that, take into consideration the following questions, the ones I asked before.

- Do you like his work?
- Do you think he has talent?
- Is the price reasonable?
- Do you have a place to put it?

If the answer is "yes" to all of the above, choose the work you like the best, the one the fits most with your home and then do what you can to help him promote his work. You might also want to talk to him about the advantages of poverty and show him how grateful he should be for his meager circumstances.

For instance:
- He doesn't have to worry about the stock market. He owns no stocks.
- No one will ever kidnap him and hold him for ransom.
- His friends will be his friends for who he is and not be trying to use him.
- He doesn't have to polish his silver.
- He won't need to worry about the reliability of hired help these days.

- He can't be black mailed.
- Will not be subject to great losses from theft.

Of course, he can always argue that being poor is not all that great and I think we'd all agree. But there is almost always a way to put a positive spin on things.

You Want to Impress People

First question I'd ask is "Why do you want to impress people?" If they're your friends you've already impressed them with who **you** are. Maybe you think that if you impress people, they will like you. You want people to like you there's one little thing my mother used to say. "If you want a friend, BE a friend."

Come on. If they don't like you now, the purchase of a painting ain't gonna do it. Ask yourself if you can think of any reason to like someone because they own a painting, a boat, or a cool car. Maybe you think you do, but subtract the painting, boat or car and if you still like the person, then you really do like the person. Subtract those things and you don't care for the person, then you really liked the painting, boat or car. So they weren't really your friend anyway, now were they?

If it's your boss, are you sure you want to change your lifestyle for a job? Are you contemplating art as a means to an end? Shouldn't you be true to yourself? But let's look at the reasons you might want to impress others:

- You're hoping to snag a mate.
- You think it might help you get a promotion.
- You want people to think you're "cultured."

Now if you're looking to snag a mate, a painting should not be the deciding factor. If you do find a person who falls in love with you, (and you with them) artwork will not seal the deal. Now you may "get lucky" if you invite someone to come look at your etchings, but a cup of coffee offered at the right time will do just as well and not cost nearly as much. Your character, your personality, those are the things that count. And the mate who is basing his or her selection of you on the fine art in your collection is not worth having.

If you think your next promotion is riding on impressing the boss, you'll need to select carefully. What does the boss like? If you manage to find something truly snazzy might it not make el bosso think you don't need a promotion or a raise? Shouldn't it be more impressive if you do an excellent job?

All that aside, if you are dead set on impressing the impresario of your work life, get yourself a bit of knowledge about the art world. Start by visiting galleries in the upscale parts of town. Read current news articles and magazines. Find something you can live with and ask the gallery owner about meeting the artist. (Always make sure the artist is still alive before you ask for a meeting. It's bad form to request an appointment with the dead.) If you do get to meet the artist, you can use the meeting as just another bragging point with the boss.

Course, once you make a selection that you feel will truly astound, amaze and galvanize your employer to the extent that a promotion will be offered; you've got to make sure it's seen. So you'll have to put together a soiree of some sort. This will mean invitations, hors d'ouevres, other guests, etc. You may spend more on the festivities than a raise will net over the next two years. Think it over.

If you're looking to convince others that you're cultured, the right accoutrements might help. The fine music in the background, the upscale decor, the subtle fragrance wafting through your suite to set off your recently purchased and suitably framed artwork. So now others will think you're refined.

What does that do for you? Do you get money for it? Does it keep you warm at night? Does it give you a cozy feeling? What?

My advice: Don't worry about what others think. As long as you like yourself, everything should turn out all right. You are the most important person in your life. Your opinion of yourself should be the single most significant input you consider as you go about living your life.

Your Walls Look Bare

Well, there you are. You've just moved into a new apartment. The furniture has been delivered but the walls look stark and bare. You need something to make your home look like a home. After you positioned the obligatory photos of family and friends, there is still too much blank space.

If you're looking for a picture of some sort, think about those categories you've been learning about. What is your favorite? Some galleries specialize in scenic paintings you might like if you're really into Category 1. If you want just a bit of color to relieve the plain pale walls, look at your furniture, what kind of colors and subject matter will enhance your surroundings? Maybe you'd prefer something non-subjective that relieves the boredom of the walls but stirs no controversy.

If you have kind of a rustic taste in decorating, a painting of a swan wearing a tutu will never work. Some galleries will let you take a painting to your home to see how it looks on your walls. That might work for you.

Just be sure that whatever you choose, it goes with what you already have in your home and that is something you can live with.

You Want to Make an Investment

For this, you need to talk to someone who is an expert.
I've never made an investment in anything in my life. But
there are magazines, books and web sites devoted to such
a thing. I personally can't imagine buying art for the sole
purpose of making a profit. There are people who do that,
I am sure, but it's not a subject on which I can share any
expertise. My only advise here is to ask someone else.

The Painting That Haunts You

You see a painting and it fascinates you. You keep going back to look at it. You can't get it out of your head. This is the best of all reasons to purchase a work of art. The artist is communicating; you have received the message.

When I go to an art show of any sort, I look for the pieces that impress me with their skill, the creativity, the approach I would not have considered, the medium used in a new way or the way the color shimmers. Were I of unlimited means, there would be no bare space on any of my walls.

If you can afford it and have a place to put it, the painting that haunts you is the one you should have and the most important reason of all for buying a painting.

Chapter 3 Quiz - Buying Art

Just like before, this is open book and the answers are in the back. Have fun.

1. The reasons for buying art include the following
   a. You have a hole in the wall
   b. You just like to spend money
   c. You want to make a good return on your investment.
   d. All of the above.
   e. A and C only.

2. If there is blood spatter on the wall from your last murder, you should move.
   a. True
   b. False
   c. All of the above.

3. The advantages of poverty include which of the following:
   a. Fluctuations in the stock market do not affect you.
   b. You cannot be blackmailed
   c. You don't have to polish the silverware.
   d. All of the above.

4. Buying a work of art is always a good idea if you want to impress someone.
   a. True
   b. False

5. A stud finder is a red dress
   a. True
   b. False

6. Before you ask to meet an artist you should
   a. Buy at least one piece of the artist's work.
   b. Know something about the artist
   c. Make sure the artist isn't dead.
   d. None of the above.

7. If you wish to invest in art, my comprehensive guide to wise investment will be helpful.
   a. True
   b. False

8. When considering a piece of art to add to your décor, which of the following are true?
   a. Color should not be a consideration.
   b. You should choose a work that works with your current domicile.
   c. Always consult your tarot cards before making a selection.
   d. Make sure it will fit in the space you have available.
   e. B and D only.

9. Always buy art to impress others regardless of your own preferences.
   a. True
   b. False

Myself, The Artist

I did not start out trying to make a career out of art. At the tender age of about 65, it finally dawned on me that it was what I had to do. Up until that point, I had worked at "fitting" or being "normal" and it had not worked out well.

Oh, I had managed to support myself. My complete resume reads almost like a dictionary of occupations. I have been employed as a bean picker, a blueberry raker, a sardine packer, a maid, a waitress, a bartender, taxi driver, sign painter, secretary, receptionist, auto detailer, masseuse, a porno movie projectionist, and a document control coordinator. I became an aviation electronics technician in the US Navy, was at one time a corporate secretary for a non-profit organization and have worked as a bookkeeper. In addition, I've had the experience of being homeless. There's more, but I'd rather not put you to sleep.

Naturally, I had considered "art" as a possibility. However, although I took a few courses here and there, I never actually majored in art and thought it would be foolishness to try to make a living from it. Nonetheless, I always had some project or other going. I wrote stories that I illustrated, made costumes and even did singing telegrams. So, without an education in art, I kept making the effort to live like a regular person, little realizing that we are all "regular" in our own unique way. Moreover, I am "normal" for me, just as you are for you. I hope that wisdom will come with age. (sigh)

Being a very practical person, I long considered my art as a foolish vanity of little value. After all, what can you do with art besides cover the hole in the wall? I did think about it a lot, though. I went to galleries and museums trying to soak it up, understand what this art stuff was all about.
At last, I realized, that for me, art is my soul. It is the manifestation of my interior and it does have a purpose. Just listen to the news someday.

Sound like a non sequitur? Not really. I pay attention to the life that goes on outside my door. The news is always filled with such angst and sorrow. Wars, diseases, political scandals and desperate causes are common fodder. Rarely news about the arts, stories about literature, music and theatre. It is depressing.

To me, Art, in all its forms is the icing on the cake, the yummy part of life. It helps to provide surcease from the negativity we encounter in our everyday world of work and the effort required to ensure that we have what we need to survive. We need art to help maintain balance and in my personal view we should, as a civilization, put just a bit more emphasis on the good stuff.

So how do we do that? A couple of decades ago, I read a book entitled "Tao Te Ching" and one passage stuck with me. *"The named is the mother of ten thousand things. The nameless is the beginning of heaven and earth."* It seems to me that the "namelessness" is what art is all about.

By "namelessness" I mean the wonder of feeling the difference in the air after a rain, or the smell of fresh sheets air dried in spring air. It's a gorgeous sunset or the feel of holding hands with someone you love. The things that cannot be defined with words. Photographs will not do it justice. Video is pointless. That "something" cannot be named. I feel that it is the artist's responsibility to draw a circle around that "namelessness."

It is a great challenge and a great joy to craft an image that will, for a moment, suspend ordinary reality for the viewer. I don't know how to make that happen. I only know what happens to me when I approach my work. Often it is as though I am falling into the paper or canvass and no longer truly exist as an individual but am instead one with the surface and the medium.

I admit it. I am besotted by these experiences. I am also fortunate that with Social Security, I am able to live reasonably well and still have the funds for paper, ink, sequins and feathers. Therefore, whether it sells or not, I cannot be stopped. I will create until I die, for I am an artist.

Please note: Ten per cent of all profit from the sale of this book will be donated to dental care for the homeless. Having been homeless myself, I know how important good dental care can be. There are those among us who seem to think that all a homeless person has to do is just go get a job. It is not that simple. Without an address, what do you put on the application? How do you manage to bathe if you have no home? Or get your clothes washed? And if you have dental problems like missing teeth or black decay showing, do you really think you'll make it through the interview process? Thus my donation for I am indeed a most fortunate person.

The Final Test

This is your final. If you manage to pass this test with 15 or more correct answers, you can consider yourself successful and carry with you the reward you will find further on.

1. Category 1 (Controlled Somethingness) might also be called...
   a. Realistic portrayal of an actual scene, object or person.
   b. A picture of something
   c. Identifiable
   d. All of the above
   e. A and C only.

2. Category 3 (Controlled Nothingness) is
   a. Usually a landscape painting
   b. Always realistic
   c. Not recognizable as anything that exists
   d. A and B
   e. C and A only
   f. All of the above

3. Category 4 (Uncontrolled Nothingness) is
   a. Nearly the same as Category 1
   b. Nearly the opposite of Category 1
   c. The favorite technique of Norman Rockwell
   d. None of the above
   e. All of the above

4. Category 2 (Uncontrolled Somethingness)
    a. It is a picture of something.
    b. It is closely related to Category 1
    c. Can be an artist's impression of reality
    d. All of the above.
    e. A and C only.

5. Which Category is also called "Controlled Nothingness?"
    a. Category 1
    b. Category 2
    c. Category 3
    d. Category 4

6. Uncontrolled Somethingness is also known as
    a. Category 1
    b. Category 2
    c. Both a. and b.
    d. Neither a. nor b.

7. A stud finder is a sexy red dress
    a. True
    b. False

8. If there is blood spatter on the wall from your last murder, you should move.
    a. True
    b. False
    c. All of the above.

9. What number is the phrase "Manneristically ethereal exhibition?
    a. 2-1-3
    b. 8-8-9
    c. 8-7-9
    d. 4-5-6

10. How many phrases can be made with a Buzz Phrase Generator?
    a. 173
    b. 1000
    c. 100
    d. 10

11. The phrase 2-3-9 is
    a. Distinctively qualitative dimensionality
    b. Dynamically egalitarian composition
    c. Dynamically egalitarian exhibition
    d. Excitingly didactic perspective

12. What phrase number is principally esoteric work?
    a. 9-7-3
    b. 3-3-9
    c. 2-2-5
    d. 7-2-5

13. What phrase number is quintessentially explorative manifestation?
    a. 0-8-3
    b. 0-2-1
    c. 0-9-1

d. 0-9-3

14. The reasons for buying art include the following
    a. You have a hole in the wall
    b. You just like to spend money
    c. You want to make a good return on your investment.
    d. All of the above.
    e. A and C only.

15. If there is blood spatter on the floor from your last murder, you should purchase a large heavy sculpture.
    a. True
    b. False
    c. All of the above.

16. The advantages of poverty include which of the following:
    a. Fluctuations in the stock market do not affect you.
    b. You cannot be blackmailed
    c. You don't have to polish the silverware.
    d. All of the above.

17. Buying a work of art is always a good idea if you want to impress someone.
    a. True
    b. False

18. Before you ask to meet an artist you should
    a. Buy at least one piece of the artist's work.
    b. Know something about the artist
    c. Make sure the artist isn't dead.

d. None of the above
19. The author of this book has worked at which of the following jobs?
    a. Bean picker
    b. Blueberry raker
    c. Sardine packer
    d. Maid
    e. Waitress
    f. Secretary
    g. Receptionist
    h. Aviation Electronics Technician
    i. Taxi Driver
    j. Sign Painter
    k. Masseuse
    l. Porno movie projectionist
    m. Auto Detailer
    n. Corporate Secretary
    o. Bookkeeper
    p. Bartender
    q. All of the above
    r. None of the above
20. The author of this book donates money to which cause?
    a. The Injured Cat Society
    b. The Starving Artist Consortium
    c. Dental Care for the Homeless
    d. Mothers Against Fathers

The Answers

Chapter 1 Quiz - Categories of Art

1. The correct answer is d.
2. C
3. B
4. D
5. C
6. A
7. C
8. B
9. B
10. B
11. Any answer is correct.

Chapter 2 Quiz - Talking about Art

1. The answer is C
2. B
3. C
4. D
5. C
6. Surprise, any answer is correct
7. Another "can't miss" question. Whatever you wrote down is correct.

Chapter 3 Quiz - Buying Art

1. E
2. A
3. D
4. B
5. B
6. C
7. B
8. E
9. B

The Final Test

1.	D
2.	C
3.	B
4.	D
5.	C
6.	B
7.	B
8.	A
9.	C
10.	B
11.	C
12.	D
13.	C
14.	E
15.	A
16.	D
17.	B
18.	C
19.	Q
20.	C

Your Reward

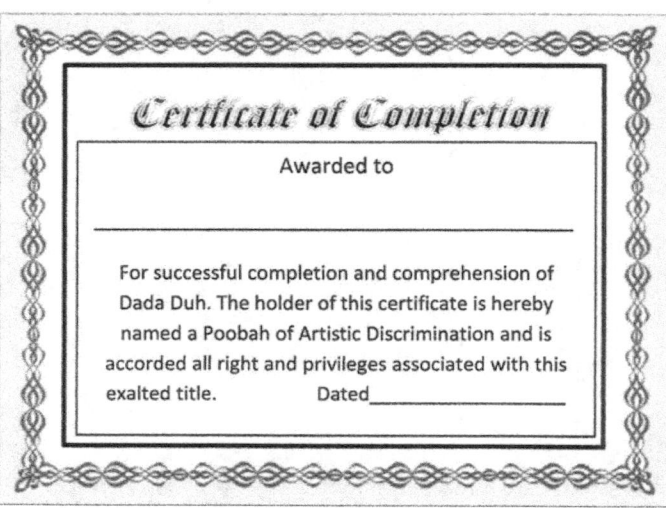

You may complete this certificate, cut it out and carry it in your wallet for maximum impact.

Index